Sandpaper Tongue Parchment Lips

poems by

Melanie Hyo-In Han

Finishing Line Press
Georgetown, Kentucky

Sandpaper Tongue Parchment Lips

Copyright © 2021 by Melanie Hyo-In Han
ISBN 978-1-64662-658-8 First Edition
All rights reserved under International and Pan-American Copyright Conventions. No part of this book may be reproduced in any manner whatsoever without written permission from the publisher, except in the case of brief quotations embodied in critical articles and reviews.

ACKNOWLEDGMENTS

I am deeply grateful to the editors of the following publications in which these individual poems first appeared:

Among Worlds Magazine: "Can I Roll, Slice, Stack Memories?" and "My Dear Yeast"
Anti-Heroin Chic: "Holding On"
Fathom Mag: "Morogoro, Tanzania"
Flora Fiction: "But This Is a Pain I Enjoy"
Lights and Shadows: "A Mistake"
Memory House Magazine: "Goodbye, Raven, Goodbye"
Red Planet Magazine: "You Had Spent Your Entire Life in One Home"
The Blue Nib: "To Miss Tranquist" and "Ukombozi Hospital"
The Idiom: "My Childhood Alphabet"
The Lyric Magazine: "Dar es Salaam Delicacies"
Thimble Magazine: "About Acacias"
Valiant Scribe: "Onslaught"

Publisher: Leah Huete de Maines
Editor: Christen Kincaid
Cover Art and Design: Sora Yi
Author Photo: Emmanuel Roussel

Order online: www.finishinglinepress.com
also available on amazon.com

Author inquiries and mail orders:
Finishing Line Press
PO Box 1626
Georgetown, Kentucky 40324
USA

Table of Contents

Waiting for Water 1

Morogoro, Tanzania 3

About Acacias 5

My Dear Yeast 6

To Miss Tranquist 7

Ukombozi Hospital 8

Can I Roll, Slice, Stack Memories? 9

My Childhood Alphabet 10

Holding On 11

Goodbye, Raven, Goodbye 13

Language Miracle 15

A Mistake 17

You Had Spent Your Entire Life in One Home 19

But This Is a Pain I Enjoy 21

Onslaught 23

Dar es Salaam Delicacies 25

Waiting for Water

Burning plastic;
trash day. Pungent,
acrid, and toxic,
just like these
stagnant ponds.
Finding water
here in Morogoro
has become tough.
What had started as
half a mile
has turned into
three miles
of dragging feet.
I leave dusty trails
along the way with
red-dirt heels
that have cracked
like the ground.

Already a snaking
line at the well
under the burning
sun of noonday.
Sitting on my
empty jerry-cans,
I wait.

First pump of water,
goes straight into
my burning mouth,
a splash onto my feet
a trickle for my head.
Up, down, up, down.
My jerry-cans
fill up, and just as
people behind me
start yelling *haraka*!
I am done.

Walking home
is a long stretch;
precious drops
of water slosh out
as I quicken
my pace
but Mom needs
me back to start
cooking *ugali*
and *sukuma wiki*
before Dad returns.

These cans,
heavy and laden.
My heart hungers
for the day
when the rains
will fall aplenty
and drown this
out. It is
god-awful.

Morogoro, Tanzania

1999, a drought with a capital D
we prayed and prayed
for the rains to fall
but it didn't for days
that stretched into weeks
that stretched into months

and i lay there
on the ground with one ear
against the pounding
heat of the land
drowned out by the
pounding of my heart

sandpaper tongue
parchment lips
dry and cracked
where life had given up
and succumbed
too weary to continue

and on tuesdays
he would come
with a wheelbarrow
rusty and laden
with the world
that creaking, crying wheelbarrow

searching
collecting then carrying
out a mound of skin and bones
children
who at least no longer felt
that thirst

and
eventually
His pain tore the skies back
and His tears became
our life as life began to spring up again and
that Drought ended

but i can still hear the creaking
and the crying, see the
image that is seared, no,
scorched in my mind
forever
that tuesday wheelbarrow

About Acacias

Acacia trees are most commonly found in Africa's savannas. They stand alone, upright, tall, and leafy, casting shade on giraffes—an escape of noonday Serengeti heat. The darkness of the wood contrasts sharply against the wide, green leaves that photosynthesize eagerly in the brutal African sun; light courses through their stringy veins. Their branches have thorns, two inches long. When they shed, it is impossible to walk near them. The thorns pierce shoes like lions' teeth pierce the necks of baby gazelles. Weaver birds weave homes amongst the tops, avoiding thorns, making shelter where shelter shouldn't be made. After the rainy season, the trees produce small flowers, bright yellow like the papyrus warbler. When the flowers are fried, they taste of honey. That night, you really wanted those honey flowers, so I decided to brave the thorns. You didn't notice my speckled, red feet.

My Dear Yeast

She says to me
"*Everyone* needs to learn."
It too hard. I too old. I try
communicate with Granddaughter
doesn't learn language of mother
because she already speak English
Universal language.

"My dear Yeast,
It is prized catch mother hen
ignorance special bond.
I grab the hem of mother,
watching while trembling. Show me
your fertilized love giggles.
Love, *Halmoni.*"

To Miss Tranquist

I wonder what you might be thinking, looking at the little Asian girl with dark hair and darker eyes in a sea of blonde hair and blue eyes. Your head does a 30 degree tilt as you pause at what I am sure must be my name.

"Uhhhh, Hai-o een?"
"It's H-yo In."
"Ah, okay, thank you."

Your face relaxes, mouth slackening as you move down the roster and see other names you can pronounce.

And throughout the school year, you somehow always seem to find someone else to call on even when I shoot my hand up before anyone else in the class, and maybe you don't think I notice, but I'm the only student you never say "Hello" to by name.

I wish you'd try.

You were the reason behind my many fights with my parents who kept insisting "Hyo In" was a beautiful name, but I didn't care that it meant "wisdom from dawn" or that it represented my family, my heritage, my culture, my language. All I ever wanted was to be called on without hesitation and be greeted every day by name.

It's been over fifteen years since I started going by "Melanie," a name that means "dark," because that's what I am to you. You can finally say it without feeling embarrassed; I hear it often and from the lips of many people, and I guess I like it.

But at what cost?

Ukombozi Hospital

Bright. Fluorescent lights, blinking on
and off. Arhythmic. Disinfectant.
Punching acidity, too clean.
Sirens. In and out. In and out. Wailing.
A woman whose son was mauled
by a rabid dog. Stitches. 38 of them.
Dad brings over a plate of cafeteria fries.
Cold, soggy, greasy. Ketchup dripping
down the edge. Blood, dripping down
Mom's forehead. Shattered trust
with the echo of shattering glass
on tile as she slipped down, sinking.
Blood, pooling. Puddling. I flinch
at Dad's heavy hand on my shoulder,
weight in his words of empty promises.
"We won't ever come back here again."
Words. They can't heal. I shrug
his hand away. I refuse to look at him.

Can I Roll, Slice, Stack Memories?

Hustle and bustle of lunchtime at Myeongdong Market. Fried chicken feet splayed out and curled at the ends, rows of hanging chilis in different shades of summer sunset, dried whole squids piled flat on top of one another, every tentacle preserved and intact. My eyes come to rest on a little pyramid of *kimbap*.

The predictable pattern of roll, slice, stack. Roll, slice, stack. The *kimbap* lady is about my mom's age, same short, dark hair turning silver, apron wrapped around her once-slim waist, and suddenly, I'm staring at my mom standing at the kitchen counter of the house that we lived in when I was eight and insecure.

4 AM she packs my lunch for a school picnic. I get up not too long after, unable to contain my excitement. Will they be impressed? Maybe even a little jealous of my mom's Korean cooking? Probably both.

But when lunchtime finally rolled around and the *kimbap* container was opened, all I heard were the quiet "Eww"s as I felt the slight shift of people moving away from me. My shaking hands found themselves tossing the *kimbap* into the open and hungry mouth of the trash can.

Their perfectly triangled white sandwiches, perfect pale skin, perfect light eyes (they looked easy enough to gouge out). Sunshine rested in their golden hair while night and fury nested in mine. Did I want to die or be white?

At home, that afternoon, I shut myself in the bathroom scrubbing my skin raw and crying my eyes dry until exhaustion called my name. The front door clicked and I threw angry words at my mom.
She never made *kimbap* again. And I avoided Korean food.

But, I find myself in a trance, walking over to the lady and handing her a 1,000 won bill, receiving a roll of *kimbap* in return. My tongue is momentarily stunned as it remembers long forgotten flavors. All I taste is salt as I pull out my phone and dial for my mom.

My Childhood Alphabet

African women on the busy, bustling streets of Harare bearing
Babies on their hips, wearing
Colorful *kangas* around their waists – orange, blue, and green –
Daring and bold like the beaded necklaces of a proud Maasai queen,
Every shade of the spectrum plays hide-and-seek in the fabrics' swirl.
Far away from the center of town children play and twirl,
Girls sit under trees, clutching dolls made of *mwarubaini* leaves.
Hidden amongst the bushes, several boys watch, silent as thieves,
Intrigued and curious, trying to figure out their foreign, female games.
Just a few feet away, their friends run around, calling each other's names,
Kicking a ball made of plastic bags,
Laughing without a care in the world even though they're dressed in rags.
Men sit around inside,
Not wanting to leave the coolness of their huts for the outside
Opting for laziness in the heat of the day,
Preferring to let their wives work and obey
Questioning their values when they complain.
Rolling up joints, indoors they remain,
Smoking miraa,
Taking in large quantities of illegally brewed changa
Until they can no longer tell apart
Vision from an actual work of art.
What it all comes down to is the sad reality in which they exist,
Xylophonic echoes of what they want and insist.
Yearning for lives filled with peace and perfection
Zambians and Zimbabweans, all alike, searching for some sort of direction.

Holding On

in the house at
6°46'43.121"S
39°15'51.031"E
i was sexually assaulted
for the first time
but i didn't know
how to tell my parents
so the boy continued
to come over to play

                              and in the house at
                                 6°43'42.651"S
                                 39°14'13.59"E
                            my mom got cancer
                              then got depressed
                        then tried to kill herself
                                but i didn't know
                          how to be there for her
                    so i disappeared to escape

and in the house at
6°44'50.505"S
39°16'41.829"E
i heard a splash at night
but i didn't know what to do
so when i found a body
facedown in the pool
bloated and purple
i threw up and sobbed

and in this house at
42°24'0.033"N
70°59'40.553"W
i realized that i never had
a normal childhood
but i didn't want to believe it
so i lied to myself
to feel better
for just a little longer

Goodbye, Raven, Goodbye

I saw a raven the other day, and the way its wings gleamed
in the sun reminded me of how your hair used to change
from blue to green to purple and back.

You had the most stunning hair: thick, silky, straight, so black
it caught the light and played tricks with it when you moved.
"It's *chal-lang chal-lang*," Grandma, whose hair you inherited,
would boast.

I ended up with Dad's hair: thin, tangled, stringy, not quite
black, but a muted brown, reminding our relatives of a *malgalgi*,
the mane of a sick horse. Koreans are rude like that sometimes.

You taught me how to French braid, Dutch braid, fishtail, waterfall,
thinking I wanted to learn to do my own hair,
but I just enjoyed touching, brushing, and playing with yours.

So on that morning when I walked into your room with Dad,
it wasn't your papery skin or your cheeks, your eyes or your arms
that made me run outside. It was your head.

Where your thick, silky, straight, and jet black hair
should have been, there was only the reflection
of the room's bright and fluorescent overhead lights.

Even though Dad told me not to, I went home that day, dug
through our kitchen drawers for the largest pair of scissors,
then, I hacked away at my hair, chopping off 12 or 13 inches

of it, reflection blurred by tears. If you couldn't have hair,
I didn't want it either. My long hair deserved an end,
your life didn't deserve the same.

I still make the big chop once my hair gets to the length
that it was during the summer of 2008, the year
that everything changed: your hair, my hair, your life, my life.

I often find myself looking for ravens and watching their
wings shimmer. My hair has gotten long again.
I swear it grows faster each time, knowing I'll say goodbye.

Language Miracle

I came home
from school one day
and you were gone.
Mom said it was because
you missed Grandpa and
you missed Korea and
you didn't wait for me
because you were bad
at saying goodbyes,
but I knew better.
You left because
you were fed up
with me, fed up
with trying
to teach Korean
to a granddaughter
who kept refusing.
So you went
back to your homeland,
a land I didn't feel
was my home,
with nothing but
6,381 miles, 12 hours
on the plane, and
hurt between us.

"My Dear Yeast,
You know I grow up in Korea while Japan abuse
forbid speak our language as child force learn
Japanese language of oppress and change
my name to other country. Yoshiko, they call me.
Many word gone when release from Japan.
Japan burn thousand and thousand book
force study Japan forbid our language
prison for people who wrote our words.
Release from Japan regain our language miracle.
I proud of my people my movement regain
history country culture. Yeast, grow up
in foreign country no use our language.
And what do you know about war for our country?
Last wish for Yeast. Learn language.
Love,
Halmoni"

A Mistake

because i wasn't ready to share
that much of myself with you

but you thought you had the right
to come and
        peer into
                tear into
                      search
thoroughly
my body
when i had said no
that, at that moment, i had things i needed
to
              hide
      from you
      from the world

you forced me to surrender to you
holding me
down
though i struggled against you

                      i was too weak

so you pried my lips apart
sucking until i was bone dry

from you probing
              prodding
                          poking
you   broke
me and you reveled in it

the sound of your ringing laughter making me sick
all over again
        sick all over again

you had dug
straight through me
leaving me an empty shell
                regretting you

You Had Spent Your Entire Life in One Home:

your mom's run-down condo in sleepy Antrim, New Hampshire where you grew up eating inauthentic General Tso's chicken at Ginger House and picking up sesame bagels with cream cheese at Audrey's on Wednesdays,

knowing
everything
about your town,
your home, which step
in your staircase creaked,
the exact shape of the burn
mark on the left side of your fridge.

        The mahogany closet in your basement where you used to curl up at age 4 to play hide-and-seek with your three sisters, the bookshelf you broke then repaired at age 10, the army green quilt you received from your grandma at age 13 that covers the twinbed in your room, in your home, in your town.

By the time I met you I had lived in over 25 places in

Korea				England
	Tanzania			
	South Africa			
	Kenya			
			Lithuania	
Chile		U.S.A.		

Some homes, some houses,

      never
      knowing

the houses
    I lived
I was packing   unpacking,
      readjusting   new places.

           thrill of leaving   Cockroach House,
    bittersweet   goodbye   Mango Tree House,
        Jacaranda House, the comings   goings
    formings   memories,   never   feeling
        rootedness.

And maybe that's why we had to end our relationship:
I was a home to you, but you were just a house to me.

**But This is a
Pain I Enjoy:**

white hot
needles, tingling
first my right foot,
then my legs as
scalding water
swirls greedily
around my belly
and my chest,
finally closing
a hand around
my throat as
I sink. I think
about the irony
of me in this
claw-foot tub
soaking in artificial
eucalyptus oil
as real, live
eucalyptus trees
char to ash,
their oils igniting
and releasing
waves of fire.

And if I really
tried hard and
remembered
the memories
I blocked out
of the many
droughts I
lived through
as a child
and the fires
I put out
as a teen,
I would maybe
do something
more, but
right here,
I just drop
beneath the
silence of the
still water.

Onslaught

February

"Hyo-In, your dad and I think you should cancel your trip to Morocco."
"No, Mom, we've already booked everything. We'll be fine, we're all young and healthy."

March

Boston—Lisbon—Madrid—Marrakech: Getting lost in the windy streets of the medina while photographing intricate designs of zillij tiles mosaicing the Old City. Unplugged. Camel trekking through the Sahara Desert and sandboarding in the dunes during sunset. Unaware. Staring at the Milky Way from our Berber campsite, sipping on mint tea. Unaffected.

Fes—Chefchaouen—Tangier: Whispering "corona, corona" fake coughing at me   ushering siblings out of my way
spitting in my direction
                          hitting me with cardboard boxes,
yelling at me to "go back to where you came from."

Tangier—Madrid—Lisbon—Boston: Wary travelers wearing masks.

Sudden barrage of information: "Covid-19." "Coronavirus." "Restaurants closed." "Parks closed." "Beaches closed." "Stay at home. Wash your hands."

"The College has made the difficult decision to transition all in-person classes to online learning for the remainder of the spring term."

> "Babe, I got laid off. Sorry."
> "Oh, no! What are we going to do?"
> "It's okay. I'm sure we'll figure out a way to pay rent."

"Hyo-In, your dad and I got kicked out of the grocery store today because the locals didn't want 'virus spreaders' shopping with them."

> "CDC."   "Unemployment."

"Although we have been thinking creatively about meaningful tasks to keep the office busy, unfortunately, we may not have enough remote work to keep you all over the coming weeks."

"Deaths."   "WHO."

April

"Maximum capacity."   "Rising death tolls."
   "Stay at home." "Shortage of masks." "Wash your hands."
         "Mass burials." "We don't know when this will end."

Dar es Salaam Delicacies

Nose pressed up against the window, I wait
for pitter-patters to turn to pelting poundings
as hundreds of flying ants rise upward,
dizzying my eyes and swarming my head.

So predictable: Tanzanian rainy seasons.

"Dad! Come on!" and he brings them as always:
bright yellow boots and clashing pink raincoat
with words on them I can't yet read, words that
Mom says I'll learn in school next year.

Tupperware in hand, I rush out,
dancing to a chorus of wings: a flapping frenzy.
Within minutes, I have plenty of the squirming creatures,
my prized possessions, enough to make Mom proud.

Back at home, the three of us busy ourselves.
Dad hangs up my dripping raincoat while
I tug away at endless wings while
Mom heats up the stove and readies

a drizzle of oil, a handful of flying ants, a pinch of salt;
sizzling in the pan, they fry quickly.
Then, around the table, Mom, Dad, and I sit,
munching and crunching our seasonal snack.

So predictable: Tanzanian rainy seasons.

And even though I lived through many of them,
I can no longer recall whether the flying ants
tasted more like bacon bits or burnt popcorn.
So I wait, nose pressed up against the window.

With Thanks

This poetry collection wouldn't exist without the help of so many people who believed in my work and supported me every step of the way.

To my 엄마, 아빠, 할머니, and 할아버지, 항상 믿어주시고 사랑해주셔서 감사해요.

To my professors and mentors at Gordon College who fueled my desire to write, especially Moisés Park, Mark Stevick, Lori Ambacher, and Graeme Bird, I hope you know how grateful I am for each of you.

To Rajiv Mohabir, Daniel Tobin, Maria Koundoura, Jabari Asim, Livia Meneghin, Richard Haney-Jardine, and Porsha Olayiwola who, among many other faculty and classmates at Emerson College, has challenged me, encouraged me, and asked me difficult questions, thank you for pushing me and for giving me the confidence to write.

To my dearest friends who are like family, specifically Corinne Wilder, Anna Yeo, Kelsie Puttbach, Jihoon Song, Dilanjan Anketell, Danny Bizumuremyi, Nate D'Andre, and Kuo Lu, thanks for being a part of my life and for being excited for my writing with every accomplishment, big and small.

To Gloria Song and Sora Yi, 진짜 너희 같은 친구들은 없다! RVA 에서부터 지금까지 쭉 응원해줘서 고마워!

And last but certainly not least... to Emmanuel Roussel, my best friend—I couldn't have done this without you. I thank you and I love you.

Melanie Hyo-In Han, born in Korea and raised in East Africa, has been calling Boston "home" for the past several years where she is a poet, teacher, and author of *Sandpaper Tongue, Parchment Lips*. Nominated for a Pushcart Prize, her poetry has received awards from "Boston in 100 Words" and *The Lyric Magazine*. Han's work has been published in *The Blue Nib, Among Worlds Magazine, Entropy,* and elsewhere.

Her degrees include a B.A. in English, Spanish, and Linguistics, and an M.Ed. in English and Spanish from Gordon College. She earned her M.F.A. in Poetry and Translation from Emerson College where she taught in the Writing Studies Program and served as an ELL Consultant. She is currently a poetry editor at *Flora Fiction*.

As a TCK (Third Culture Kid), the inspiration behind her poetry comes from her own childhood experiences and an exploration of identity, belonging, and culture through the use of fragmented form and inclusion of multiple languages. She also writes nonfiction and does translation work between English, Spanish, and Korean. During her free time, Han enjoys visiting new countries and trying different ethnic foods with her husband.

Learn more about her at melaniehan.com.

www.ingramcontent.com/pod-product-compliance
Lightning Source LLC
LaVergne TN
LVHW040118080426
835507LV00041B/1628